To: Dal

You both are a splendid
example of many of the
Principles in this book.

I appreciate your
faithfulness to God
and the blessings you
give to others!

Bill Jacobs

# Time for
# CHRIST

## Seven Christian Principles to Help You Be a Good Steward of Your Time

### Gil Jacobs

WESTBOW
PRESS®
A DIVISION OF THOMAS NELSON
& ZONDERVAN

Unless otherwise indicated, Scripture quotations taken from
the HOLY BIBLE, NEW INTERNATIONAL VERSION.
Copyright 1973, 1978, 1984 by International Bible Society.
Used by permission of Zondervan Publishing House.

WestBow Press books may be ordered through booksellers or by contacting:

WestBow Press
A Division of Thomas Nelson & Zondervan
1663 Liberty Drive
Bloomington, IN 47403
www.westbowpress.com
1 (866) 928-1240

ISBN: 978-1-9736-6042-2 (sc)
ISBN: 978-1-9736-6044-6 (hc)
ISBN: 978-1-9736-6043-9 (e)

Library of Congress Control Number: 2019905011

Print information available on the last page.

WestBow Press rev. date:  05/14/2019

*This book is dedicated to Christ Jesus, my Lord and Savior, "who, being in very nature God … humbled himself and became obedient to death—even death on a cross" (Philippians 2:6–8) to pay the penalty for my sins (Romans 5:8) so I could have eternal life and enjoy being with Him forever.*

# Contents

Acknowledgments ................................................................ix

Introduction ......................................................................xi

CHAPTER 1: Spend Time with God ......................................1

CHAPTER 2: Our Time Should Demonstrate a Love for
Other People ....................................................11

CHAPTER 3: Be a Good Steward and Enjoy What God
Has Given You ..................................................23

CHAPTER 4: Be Trustworthy with Your Little Portions
of Time..............................................................39

CHAPTER 5: Count the Cost................................................47

CHAPTER 6: Live in Harmony with God's Plan ....................55

CHAPTER 7: Rest and Remember the Sabbath and
Keep it Holy ......................................................67

Conclusion .......................................................................77

APPENDIX A: Application and Time Log Worksheet................79

APPENDIX B: Guide for Thinking about Christ-Pleasing
Priorities ..........................................................85

About the Author................................................................89

# Acknowledgments

During my seventy-three years on this earth, God has placed many people in my path to encourage me and help me on my spiritual journey. Although I cannot name everyone, I would like to acknowledge some who have had a significant impact on my spiritual development and inspired me to write and now publish this book with the hope that it will be a help to those who seek to honor Christ with their time.

From the beginning, my parents, Ruth and Gill Jacobs, dedicated me through baptism and encouragement to become a Christian. Pastor Chell was a guide and teacher who taught and affirmed my salvation though Lutheran catechism. Then there were the dry years when I was not growing spiritually, until Bill Matthews challenged me about my offensive language, which resulted in renewing my spiritual growth through personal Bible study and church attendance.

After a series of life-changing events, I came to the

point where I needed help leading the Christian life. God responded to my prayers by bringing Chuck Fox into my life to disciple me. Since then I have been blessed with many Christian friends through joining the Gideon ministry, Christian Businessmen's Connection, and First Alliance Church. These friends include Carl Anderson, John Anderson, Dr. Ken Andryc, Clay Bannister, Bob Bowen, John Bergquist, Jim McDonald, Joel Miller, Jack Niethamer, Gary Renaud, Bob Wisener, and many more. These men demonstrate to me the truth of the verse that says, "As iron sharpens iron, so one man sharpens another" (Proverbs 27:17). I am blessed by their friendships.

Finally, my life was changed forever when I met and married the love of my life, Gail. She is truly a Proverbs 31 wife and wonderful helpmate. She makes our journey together meaningful and fun.

I thank God for all these people and the many more who have inspired me in my Christian walk.

# Introduction

B efore we start, I want to emphasize that this guide is for Christians. If you have not received Jesus Christ as your Lord and Savior, I recommend that you do not delay. Spend the time right now making that commitment. In John 3:16, we read: "For God so loved the world that he gave his one and only Son, that whoever believes in him shall not perish but have eternal life." Romans 3:23 says: "for all have sinned and fall short of the glory of God." John 1:12 declares: "Yet to all who did received him, to those who believed in his name, he gave the right to become children of God."

If you have not received Jesus Christ into your life, consider this from Revelation 3:20: "Here I am! I stand at the door and knock. If anyone hears my voice and opens the door, I will come in and eat with that person, and they with me." I commend you to make that commitment right now. Do not delay this decision. This is the most important use of your time right now! It is the most important decision of your life!

Say this simple prayer: "I am confessing to God that I am a sinner. I repent of my sins. Believing that the Lord Jesus Christ died for my sins on the cross and was raised for my justification, I do now receive and confess Him as my personal Savior. I am willing to follow Jesus Christ and obey Him."

We have assurance, because in Romans 10:9, we read, "That if you confess with your mouth, 'Jesus is Lord,' and believe in your heart that God raised him from the dead, you will be saved." If you have made this commitment, go and confess to another Christian today that you believe that Jesus Christ is your Lord and Savior. You now have assurance that you will be saved.

"For it is by grace you have been saved, through faith—and this not from yourselves, it is the gift of God—not by works, so that no one can boast" (Ephesians 2:8–9).

What is time? How should we spend our time? Whose time is it anyway? These are some of the questions I want to address in this guide.

As Christians, we must remember that we are in a spiritual battle. We will face trials. One of the common problems facing Christians is the use of their time. I have met Christians from all walks of life who are struggling with the use of their time. I could relate to them because several years ago, I felt a great deal of frustration with the demands on my time. I was working full time in a new career field. I was a husband and a father of several active teenagers. I was a leader in two local evangelism ministries as well as being on our church's finance committee. I was overcommitted. My Christian service had become a heavy burden.

I knew I was doing something wrong, because Christ said: "Take my yoke upon you and learn from me, for I am gentle and humble in heart, and you will find rest for your souls. For my yoke is easy and my burden is light" (Matthew 11:29–30).

This problem of seemingly ever-increasing demands on my time caused me to begin a search for a strategy on how to be a good steward of my time. The insights that follow are the result of that search.

Finally, I want to emphasize that when we accept God's gracious gift of eternal life through Jesus Christ, we become His adopted daughters and sons. Just as we love and care for our own children, God loves and cares for us. Once we are His sons and daughters, He promises to help us live our new lives in Christ. As we examine our lives and our relationship with our heavenly Father, we should keep in mind our own joy when our children seek to please us. Because God loved us so much and demonstrated that love to us, we now are able, with the help of the Holy Spirit, to live lives that please and glorify Him. My hope is that you will glorify God and enjoy your relationship with Him as you apply His principles of time stewardship in your life.

# CHAPTER
# ONE

## Spend Time with God

I want to begin by defining time. To me, time is a dimension, just like the physical dimensions of length, width, and depth. We usually measure time in seconds, minutes, hours, days, months, and years. Therefore, time is in every aspect of our existence. For example, there is the time value of money, there is the time of our lives, and there is the time (history) of the earth.

For human beings, the definition of time is not the real problem. The real problem or question is this: How should I invest my time? We need to recognize that we have a finite amount of time available. Each day contains only twenty-four hours. Each year contains only 365 or 366 days. An average human lifetime is currently about seventy-five years. In other words, we have a limited amount of time to invest, so we must make choices on how to invest it. For a Christian, the question is, how can I invest my time so that I will please my Lord and Savior, Jesus Christ? I want to tell you what scripture revealed to me about Christ-pleasing ways to answer this question.

First, I discovered that God's perspective on time is not one thousand years, one million years, or even one billion years. Rather, God's perspective is eternal. He is the beginning and the end, and He created the heavens and the earth and all that is in them (Revelation 10:6). On the other hand, humankind's perspective tends to be about seventy-five years because our days on earth are few (Psalm 90:10–12). Our time on earth compared to eternity is one drop of water compared to the Pacific Ocean. The psalmist writes, "Show me, Lord, my life's end and the number of my days; let me know how fleeting is my life" (Psalm 39:4).

Numerous Bible verses support the eternal truth that God's perspective is different from the human perspective. In Isaiah 55:8, we read, "'For my thoughts are not your thoughts, neither are your ways my ways,' declares the Lord." Proverbs 3:5 says, "Trust in the Lord with all your heart and lean not on your own understanding; in all your ways submit to him, and he will make your paths straight." From these verses of scripture, I came to this conclusion. For me to see time and my life from God's perspective, I need to *spend time with God* to develop my relationship with Him. This is the first time-stewardship principle scripture revealed to me.

I believe spending time with God must be my highest priority. Unfortunately, before I really understood this principle, I found myself so busy serving God that I was missing the most important use of my time. When I invited Christ into my life to be my Savior and Lord, I spent much time reading His Word and in prayer with Him. As I realized God's great love for me and experienced Him in my life, I began to serve Him in several different ministries. Unfortunately, I allowed this service and all the other activities in my life to take me away from my quiet time with God. As a result, my life began to lose balance. Like a wobbly wheel on a bicycle, my life was becoming uncomfortable.

In Luke 10:39–42, we read the story of Jesus visiting Mary and Martha.

> *She had a sister called Mary, who sat at the Lord's feet listening to what he said. But Martha was distracted by all the preparations that had to be made. She came to him and asked, "Lord, don't you care that my sister has*

*left me to do the work by myself? Tell her to help me!"*

*"Martha, Martha," the Lord answered, "you are worried and upset about many things, but only one thing is needed. Mary has chosen what is better, and it will not be taken away from her."*

Notice how Jesus commended Mary for spending time with Him.

Jesus's life on earth exemplified the importance of spending time with God. We read in Luke 5:16, "But Jesus often withdrew to lonely places and prayed." Matthew 14:23 says, "After he had dismissed them, he went up on a mountainside by himself to pray. When evening came, he was there alone." Jesus Christ during His time on earth spent time alone with His heavenly Father.

For us to bear fruit in our service to God, spending time with Christ is essential. In John 15:5, Christ said, "I am the vine; you are the branches. If a man remains in me and I in him, he will bear much fruit; apart from me you can do nothing." For us to abide in Him, we must spend time with Him.

As I examined my life, I realized that I was not spending much daily time with Christ. I was so busy serving God that I was missing the most important part. I was missing having a relationship with Him. Now I rise earlier, before my family, so that I can spend time alone with God. This time has become very important to me. It is vital to my spiritual growth. I believe that Christians have an inner longing to spend time with God. God designed us to have fellowship with Him. The psalmist writes, "As the deer pants for streams of water, so my soul pants for you, O God. My soul thirsts for God, for the living God. When can I go and meet with God?" (Psalm 42:1–2).

How much time do you spend with Christ each day? I recommend that you keep a time log for a week and see how much time you spend alone with Him. Spending time with Christ can be compared to a young person spending time with the love of his or her life. I recall my own courtship days when I would find all kinds of ways to spend time with Gail. I did this because I was so very much in love with Gail, who is now my beloved wife.

From my perspective, if you really love God, you will want to spend time with Him. Matthew 22:37 says, "Jesus replied: 'Love the Lord your God with all your heart and with all your soul and with all your mind.' This is the first and greatest commandment." Are you in love with God? If you are, you'll find ways to spend time with Him. And if you spend time with Him, you'll come to love Him even more as you discover more about Him.

# Application

On the lines below, write down how you are going to apply the principle of spending time with God. I suggest that you consider starting your day by spending seven minutes with Him. During that time I recommend that you begin with a short prayer. Read from God's Holy Word for three or four minutes and then end with time in prayer and reflection on what you have read. An easy-to-remember outline for your final prayer is the following:

**A**: adoration
**C**: confession
**T**: thanksgiving
**S**: supplication

Now ask God to give you wisdom as you write down how you plan to spend time with Him each day.

# Key Verse

Jesus replied: "Love the Lord your God with all your heart and with all your soul and with all your mind. This is the first and greatest commandment" (Matthew 22:37–38).

CHAPTER

# TWO

## Our Time Should Demonstrate a Love for Other People

The second time-stewardship principle from God's Word is that our time should *demonstrate a love for other people*. In John 15:12, Jesus said, "My command is this: love each other as I have loved you."

As I grow closer to God, I become increasingly aware of the great love He has for us. In Genesis 1:27, we read, "So God created man in his own image, in the image of God he created him; male and female he created them." God loves us, even while we were sinners. "But God demonstrates his own love for us in this: While we were still sinners, Christ died for us" (Romans 5:8).

"A new command I give you: Love one another. As I have loved you, so you must love one another. By this all men will know that you are my disciples, if you love one another" (John 13:34–35). God commands us to love one another just as Christ loved us.

> Then the King will say to those on his right, "Come, you who are blessed by my Father; take your inheritance, the kingdom prepared for you since the creation of the world. For I was hungry and you gave me something to eat, I was thirsty and you gave me something to drink, I was a stranger and you invited me in, I needed clothes and you clothed me, I was sick and you looked after me, I was in prison and you came to visit me." (Matthew 25:34–36)

Christ demonstrated His love through action. He fed the hungry. He healed the sick. He discipled the lost. He died on a cross for our sins so that we could have life everlasting. Christ demonstrated His love by action. He spent time with others. He understood and gave them what they needed. (See also Luke 6:27–31 and James 2:14–18.)

From Christ's words to us and His personal example, I believe we are to demonstrate love for other people with our time.

*This is how we know what love is: Jesus Christ laid down his life for us. And we ought to lay down our lives for our brothers. If anyone has material possessions and sees his brother in need but has no pity on him, how can the love of God be in him? Dear children, let us not love with words or tongue but with actions and in truth. This then is how we know that we belong to the truth, and how we set our hearts at rest in his presence. (1 John 3:16–19)*

Real love is demonstrated by action. It is selfless giving even to the point of sacrifice. Love is demonstrated by using our time to serve others. Throughout the Bible, God provides us with many examples of love in action.

In Song of Solomon 4:1, we read how Solomon loved his wife on their wedding night. As you read these words of adoration, think of how his wife must have felt.

"How beautiful you are, my darling! Oh, how beautiful! Your eyes behind your veil are doves. Your hair is like a flock of goats descending from Mount Gilead." Okay, today we might not want someone to liken our hair to a flock of goats, but I am sure you get the idea. (Actually, this is a beautiful metaphor because the goats of Syria are mostly black with long, silky hair.)

The point I am trying to make is that we are to demonstrate our love to the spouse that God has given us. He has entrusted us with one of His most precious creations, one of His very own daughters or sons. We need to act toward this sister or brother in Christ, accordingly. I believe that when God created woman as a companion for man, He put in the male-female relationship the potential to experience love in its fullest meaning. For this love between a husband and wife to reach its potential, they must spend time doing romantic things together, being each other's friend and companion, and selflessly serving each other. I believe this is what God intended for us. This takes time. Next to spending time with God, I believe our next highest priority should be spending time with the wife or husband God has given us. We should frequently ask ourselves, "How much time have I spent doing romantic things with my spouse this last week?" Or has golf with the guys, making money, or even some worthwhile service kept me from loving the spouse God has given me? In Ephesians 5:33 we read, "However, each one of you also must love his wife as he loves himself, and the wife must respect her husband."

Just as we are to spend time with our spouses so we

can know and love them, we need to spend time with our children. We are to love our children just as our heavenly Father has loved us. There are numerous references to our relationship with God as His children.

I especially like Proverbs 4:1–6, which says:

> *Listen, my sons, to a father's instruction; pay attention and gain understanding. I give you sound learning, so do not forsake my teaching. When I was a boy in my father's house, still tender, and an only child of my mother, he taught me and said, "Lay hold of my words with all your heart; keep my commands and you will live. Get wisdom, get understanding; do not forget my words or swerve from them. Do not forsake wisdom, and she will protect you; love her, and she will watch over you."*

Teaching God's wisdom and the application of that wisdom to our children takes time. This, in my view, is our next highest priority. Only people will last for eternity, not cars, houses, businesses, or whatever else we build on this earth.

In Revelation 21:1 we read, "Then I saw a new heaven and a new earth, for the first heaven and the first earth had passed away, and there was no longer any sea." I want my children to be with me in heaven ten thousand years from now and throughout eternity. I believe we as parents have a vital role in teaching our children so that they can be in eternity with us. (I also understand that I cannot make the ultimate choice for my children; rather, people must make their own decision to ask Jesus Christ into their hearts as their Lord and Savior. As a parent, I do have a responsibility to train and encourage them and demonstrate God's love by my actions.)

We also have a special responsibility to love our parents. God tells us to "Honor your father and your mother, as the Lord your God has commanded you, so that you may live long and that it may go well with you in the land the Lord your God is giving you" (Deuteronomy 5:16). Again, as in our other relationships, this takes time. The amount of time we spend helping our parents meet their needs will vary through the years. As our parents grow older, we have a special responsibility to spend time meeting their needs.

After our immediate family, who are the others we are to love? This question was posed many years ago to Jesus who replied by telling the story of the good Samaritan who found a stranger in distress along the road. We read about this in Luke 10:33–35.

> *But a Samaritan, as he traveled, came where*
> *the man was; and when he saw him, he took*

*pity on him. He went to him and bandaged his wounds, pouring on oil and wine. Then he put the man on his own donkey, took him to an inn and took care of him. The next day he took out two silver coins and gave them to the innkeeper. "Look after him," he said, "and when I return, I will reimburse you for any extra expense you may have."*

This is a story of love in action. I believe God calls us to love all the people He brings into our lives.

So, in summary, I believe our time should *demonstrate a love for other people.* Like ever-widening concentric circles, our lives touch other people. I believe we have a special responsibility to love the people God places closest to us. First, we are to love our spouse and children, then our parents and extended family, and then our neighbors near and far. As we examine our time and how we are using the moments God has given us, we need to make sure that we are using our time to *demonstrate love for other people for God's glory.*

# Application

In light of Jesus's command to love one another as Jesus loved us (John 15:12), how you are going to apply the principle that *our time should demonstrate a love for other people*? I suggest that you ask the Holy Spirit for guidance as you consider how to apply this principle and then write your plan below.

# Key Verse

"My command is this: Love each other as I have loved you" (John 15:12).

CHAPTER

# THREE

## Be a Good Steward and Enjoy What God Has Given You

A third Christian time stewardship principle from scripture is that we are to be *a good steward and enjoy what God has given us*. We are to be faithful stewards with the time, talent, and treasure God has entrusted in our care. "Now it is required that those who have been given a trust must prove faithful" (1 Corinthians 4:2). Especially important is the perspective that we are stewards, not the permanent owners of anything. God is the creator and owner of the universe and everything in it. We are privileged to be His stewards for a season. In other words, I believe that we should view our time, wealth, and talents as treasures entrusted to our care from God.

Jesus told a parable that helps me understand God's perspective.

> *Again, it will be like a man going on a journey, who called his servants and entrusted his property to them. To one he gave five talents of money, to another two talents, and to another one talent, each according to his ability. Then he went on his journey. The man who had received the five talents went at once and put his money to work and gained five more. So also, the one with the two talents gained two more. But the man who had received the one talent went off, dug a hole in the ground and hid his master's money.*
>
> *After a long time, the master of those servants returned and settled accounts with them. The man who had received the five talents brought the other five. "Master," he said, "you entrusted me with five talents. See, I have gained five more."*

*His master replied, "Well done, good and faithful servant! You have been faithful with a few things; I will put you in charge of many things. Come and share your master's happiness!"*

*The man with the two talents also came. "Master," he said, "you entrusted me with two talents; see, I have gained two more."*

*His master replied, "Well done, good and faithful servant! You have been faithful with a few things; I will put you in charge of many things. Come and share your master's happiness!"*

*Then the man who had received the one talent came. "Master," he said, "I knew that you are a hard man, harvesting where you have not sown and gathering where you have not scattered seed. So, I was afraid and went out and hid your talent in the ground. See, here is what belongs to you."*

*His master replied, "You wicked, lazy servant! So, you knew that I harvest where I have not sown and gather where I have not scattered seed? Well then, you should have put my money on deposit with the bankers, so that when I returned, I would have received it back with interest."*

*"Take the talent from him and give it to the one who has the ten talents. For everyone who has will be given more, and he will have an abundance. Whoever does not have, even what he has will be taken from him. And throw that worthless servant outside, into the darkness, where there will be weeping and gnashing of teeth." (Matthew 25:14–30)*

These are strong words that tell me I am accountable to God for how I use the time, talent, and wealth He gave me. "For we must all appear before the judgment seat of Christ, that each one may receive what is due him for the things done while in the body, whether good or bad" (2 Corinthians 5:10). I want God to tell me when I appear before Him at my judgment, "Well done, good and faithful servant." With the help of the Holy Spirit, I am striving to be that good and faithful servant.

A good steward knows the status of those things for which he is responsible. In Proverbs 27:23 we read: "Be sure you know the condition of your flocks, give careful attention to your herds." Because of the dynamic nature of life, I determined that I need to make an ongoing assessment of the condition of the "flock" God entrusts in my care. Of interest to me is the fact that time is a resource that is required by all the sheep in my flock. Time is also a finite resource that must be carefully allocated. We each have only 168 hours per week to allocate to the flock God has placed in our care. Our flock consists of our own physical, spiritual, social, and intellectual resources, our spouses, families, employees, neighbors, and the physical and financial resources God has entrusted to our care. Each of these places a claim on our time. How do we allocate our limited time to these many claims? First, I believe we are wise if we assess all that has a claim on our time. This is not a onetime assessment but rather a dynamic, continuing process. We need to know the status of our flock and how we are doing meeting their needs.

I want to recommend several actions that can help you know the status of your flock. First, make a list of all the people and things that have a legitimate claim on your time. (Appendix A can provide some insights as to the major categories of people and things.)

Second, spend time with the people on your list and learn from them how you are doing at meeting this responsibility. One easy way is to just ask. For example, ask someone in your circle, "What can I do to help you do your job or make your life better?"

Third, evaluate the effectiveness of your time in stewarding the physical resources that God has entrusted in your care. For example, how are you doing in performing maintenance on the family vehicles? (This is such a weak point for me that I must ask Gail to remind me.)

Fourth, try keeping a time log (see appendix A) for a week to see how you are using your time in meeting the legitimate claims on your time.

Once you know how you are doing, then you can consider whether you are being a good steward of your time. Here's an example. In December 1993, I did my own time log at the encouragement of my uncle, Dr. Ray Martin, who served God as a minister, missionary, and seminary professor. As I stated previously, I was feeling overwhelmed and heavily burdened with all my responsibilities. I followed my uncle's suggestion of keeping a time log so that I would know how I was spending my time.

At the end of that week, I discovered I was spending more than twenty hours per week in Christian service in three different ministries. Because of my leadership responsibilities in two of these ministries, I really needed more than twenty hours to do the kind of job that was needed. This situation presented a conflict between my expectations as to what needed to be done and my available time. Since I worked full time and needed to spend time with my wife and children as well as perform maintenance on our home, cars, etc., I could not continue spending twenty hours of Christian service without taking away from my other stewardship responsibilities. The way I solved this dilemma was to begin to become a better steward of my time.

By being a steward of my time, I mean I took deliberate action to manage the fixed amount of time available to me. I wanted to invest my time in ways that would please God rather than to be cast about by the winds of my circumstances. Because of this, I developed a stewardship model that helped me manage my time.

There are four key components in that model.

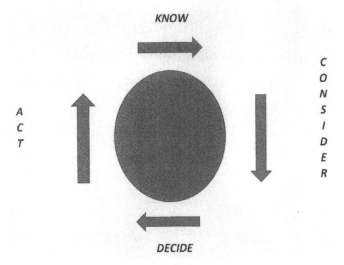

By *knowing* my responsibilities and my available resources, I was able to *consider* the situation. After prayer and discussion with my wife and other Christians, examining God's Word and considering the circumstances of upcoming elections, I decided not to run for the presidency of one of the ministries, even though I was strongly encouraged by the members to continue.

Rather, I acted to help another man transition into this leadership role. This action significantly lessened my burden. It gave me the time I needed to love and care for my family. It gave me the time to be a good steward of the other resources God entrusted in my care. It enabled

God's ministries to continue to function. I was able to invest more time and energy to one of my ministries while the new president of the other ministry was able to invest the needed time. This also helped him grow in his walk with the Lord as he used his spiritual gift of leadership and became a very good president of that ministry. From this example, I hope that you can understand the stewardship model that worked for me.

Some helpful questions that I ask myself when using this stewardship model are:

## Know

What has God entrusted in my care?

What are the legitimate claims on my time?

How am I doing as a steward of all that God has entrusted in my care?

Am I fulfilling God's guidance in Proverbs 27:23 that says: "Be sure you know the condition of your flocks, give careful attention to your herds"?

Am I leaving enough reserve in my schedule for interruptions, unexpected opportunities, or emergencies? (A good reference on this concept is *Margin* by Richard A. Swenson.)

What have I learned from my previous decisions and actions?

## Consider

What does God's Word say about this?

What do my trusted Christian advisors say about this?

What do my circumstances indicate?

What do my prayers reveal about this?

Am I at peace about this? Or has the Holy Spirit indicated something is wrong?

## Decide

What is the Holy Spirit leading me to do?

Once I am sure of God's leading, am I decisive in making a commitment to act?

## Act

Am I procrastinating, especially on unpleasant and difficult actions?

Am I a doer, not just a hearer of God's Word?

What is the best use of my time right now?

Along with being a good steward is the concept of enjoying that which God has given us. "Moreover, when God gives any man wealth and possessions, and enables him to enjoy them, to accept his lot and be happy in his work—this is a gift of God" (Ecclesiastes 5:19).

Learning to be content is one of the secrets of enjoying

what God gives us. Sometimes we want more, and this can lead to the sin of coveting what others have. It can lead to discontent. Striving after more things can cause us to miss being good stewards. For example, I see some people working overtime or two jobs to acquire more things when their children desperately need them and their time. They need their parents' guidance and love as they face the many temptations and sins in our society. These parents are missing their most important stewardship responsibility because they want more things. They are not investing in the eternal treasure that is their children. I am not speaking of the unfortunate families and single parents who have no choice and must work the long hours and two jobs just to survive. I am speaking of those who don't need to work the long hours to meet the basic needs of food, clothing, and shelter. In summary, my third Christian time stewardship principle is to *be a good steward and enjoy what God has given you.*

# Application

I suggest you think about the application of this principle by thanking God for all that He has given you. As you praise and thank God, ask Him to help you understand how you can be a good steward of all that He has entrusted in your care. Then write down how you are going **to *be a good steward and enjoy what God has given you.***

# Key Verse

"Moreover, when God gives any man wealth and possessions, and enables him to enjoy them, to accept his lot and be happy in his work—this is a gift of God" (Ecclesiastes 5:19).

CHAPTER

# FOUR

# Be Trustworthy with Your
# Little Portions of Time

A good steward is someone who can be trusted with little things as well as great things. In Luke 16:10 Christ said, "Whoever can be trusted with very little can also be trusted with much, and whoever is dishonest with very little will also be dishonest with much." This verse revealed to me a fourth Christian time stewardship principle: *be trustworthy with your little portions of time.* Just as small bricks can be used to build a valuable home, small chunks of time can be used to build a valuable part of your life.

Imagine a single red brick. By itself it is not very useful (other than to smash bugs, I suppose). In fact, if you imagine a pile of bricks, they are not very useful in that form. However, if you organize those bricks, they can be made to form a valuable home. Now imagine small chunks of time. A chunk of time equal to fifteen or thirty minutes each day by itself may not be very useful, but if you imagine 365 chunks of time equal to fifteen minutes each, you have a substantial pile of time. Now, if you organize that pile of time, you can produce something of substantial value, just as you can produce something of value by organizing a pile of bricks.

Let me give you a practical example. When I was in my thirties, I observed how men in their forties were different. Some were overweight, smoked, and demonstrated great difficulty in doing physical activities. Some even had serious heart attacks that changed their lives forever.

On the other hand, I observed men in their forties who were physically fit, ran several miles each day, and did not smoke. They seemed much younger and healthier than the other men. So I committed myself to being like the men who were physically fit. I quit smoking my pipe. I became a runner. I tried to participate in some form of exercise every day except Sunday. When I was in my forties, I became the professor of military science for ROTC at a university. Because I had maintained good physical fitness, I was able to run and do physical exercises with the university students. (I even competed with the students and experienced great fun in giving out award certificates for the physical fitness test that said "I Almost Beat the Colonel." Unfortunately, I also had to award more than a few certificates that said "I Beat the Colonel." I guess none of us can stay young forever.)

This experience emphasized the importance of being faithful with the little portions of my time. By spending an hour a day in some type of physical activity, God gave me a healthy body that was able to lead men and women, twenty-five years my junior, in physical exercise. My little acts of faithfulness were rewarded by health and physical fitness.

God's principle of being trustworthy with the little things applies to so many areas of our lives. Let me give two more examples. If a person saves and invests just a little over three dollars per day or $100 per month from age twenty-two to age sixty-two, that money will grow to a substantial amount over those forty years. (Assuming a 12 percent return on their investment each year, that money will grow to more than one million dollars in forty years.)

Now consider how much closer to God you will grow if you spend fifteen, thirty, or sixty minutes with Him each day. That investment will grow, and God will bless your time with Him. At the end of forty years of investing a little time each day with God, that investment will give you a return worth far more than one million dollars.

# Application

Reflect on your schedule and consider the little "bites" of time that are consistently available to you. For me, the fifteen minutes that I drove to work each day were valuable because I used them to listen to tapes. I started with tapes of psalms and proverbs and alternated these tapes with Promise Keeper Music and other topics of interest. Notice that I found these daily fifteen minute bites of time valuable because I used them purposefully, rather than just listening to whatever happens to be on the radio. A friend of mine started using his fifteen-minute work break to spend time alone with God. Those daily fifteen minutes add up quickly. In a year, they amount to more than sixty hours of purposeful activity that enhances our lives and our relationship with God.

Now, write down how you are going to apply the principle *be trustworthy with your little portions of time* on the space below.

# Key Verse

"Whoever can be trusted with very little can also be trusted with much, and whoever is dishonest with very little will also be dishonest with much" (Luke 16:10).

# CHAPTER
# FIVE

## Count the Cost

A fifth-time stewardship principle is found in Luke 14:28–30, where Jesus Christ taught that we are to *count the cost* before making a commitment. Jesus was specifically talking about the cost of being His disciple. We must carefully *count the cost* before adding any new activity to our lives or making any new commitments. Because our time is a finite resource, we inevitably must give something else up if we take on any new activities or responsibilities. Sometimes we are better off if we eliminate one activity for another. For example, I give up some extra sleep so I can spend time in the morning with God.

A word of caution is provided to us in Proverbs 17:1: "Better is a dry crust with peace and quiet than a house full of feasting, with strife." Contemporary society seems to be constantly running at a faster and faster pace. I recognize that I need to slow down and resist the temptation to cram too much into my life. That way, I will be able to do well my important commitments. I know I cannot do this alone; I need the power of the Holy Spirit to help me keep my life in balance. This takes constant prayer and lots of self-control (Galatians 5:22–23).

The concept of limits is an important one. As we make decisions concerning commitments, we need to recognize that we have limits. We need to act responsibly within the limits of time and other resources God has so graciously given us. We need to structure our lives so that we can act responsibly within our God-given limits. This means I must consider my limits and carefully *count the cost* before I make any commitments. I want to be sure that I can do what I say I will do. I want to be a man of my word. Just as God fulfills every word and promise that He makes, I want to fulfill my commitments.

Considering my limited resources and the vast number of needs in our world (from unsaved, poor people to my daughter's need for her father to spend time with her), I must surely *count the cost* before making any commitments.

How do I decide how much time to give to my church,

my family, my career, my personal needs, personal witnessing, the poor, and the many legitimate charitable organizations?

How do I balance using myself for God's work and using myself sensibly for the long term?

How do I know when it is appropriate to take on tasks that I cannot do in my own strength and abilities because they are urgently needed—relying on God's special, all-sufficient power to enable me?

When is it appropriate to deprive others (such as my family) of time they have a legitimate claim on to do what I perceive as God's work?

To resolve these difficult questions, we must have a relationship with the Living God who will guide and help us. James 1:5 states, "If any of you lacks wisdom, he should ask God, who gives generously to all without finding fault, and it will be given to him."

I believe God gives us wisdom through His Word, His Church, and His Holy Spirit. The principles, examples, and concepts in His Word are guideposts that will help us as we work our way through difficult and important choices on how to invest our time.

Appendix B contains a guide suggested by Dr. Ray Martin that may be helpful in thinking about Christ-pleasing priorities for the use of our time and other resources.

# Application

Read appendix B and consider your priorities and commitments. Consider your commitment to your spouse, children, church, community, and so on. Then write out how you plan to *count the cost* before adding any new commitments to your life or the cost of not changing your priorities.

# Key Verse

"Suppose one of you wants to build a tower. Will he not first sit down and estimate the cost to see if he has enough money to complete it?" (Luke 14:28)

# SIX

# Live in Harmony with God's Plan

I f you want to live the abundant life, you must live in harmony with God's plan. Jesus promised us an abundant life when He said, "The thief comes only to steal and kill and destroy; I have come that they may have life and have it to the full" (John 10:10).

How can we *live in harmony with God's plan*? We do this by being directed and empowered by the Holy Spirit. The Christ-directed life, instead of the self-directed life, is described in 1 Corinthians 2:15–16: "The spiritual man makes judgments about all things, but he himself is not subject to any man's judgment: For who has known the mind of the Lord that he may instruct him? But we have the mind of Christ."

In other words, when we spend time with Christ in His word, we will have the mind of Christ and will *live in harmony with God's plan.* When we do this, we will experience God and the abundant life that Jesus Christ promised us.

I understand that we do this by faith. It is by faith that we are filled with the Holy Spirit, and because of Jesus Christ, we can have a personal relationship with God. Through this personal, intimate relationship with God we can receive His guidance and wisdom for making the choices that direct our lives.

One way that God directs us is through His Holy Word. Another way is through our circumstances and relationships with other Christians. God speaks to us in different ways, and as He reveals where He is working, we can join Him and experience Him even more fully. When we are faithful in obeying His last command to us, I believe He rewards us by revealing even more of Himself and His plan. Through this, we can develop a deeper and more intimate relationship with God. We can experience the joy of being in His presence.

As we consider where to invest our limited time and

other resources so that we live in harmony with God's plan, I believe we need to pray continuously for wisdom. "If any of you lacks wisdom, he should ask God, who gives generously to all without finding fault, and it will be given to him" (James 1:5).

In Matthew 6:19–21, Jesus taught, "Do not store up for yourselves treasures on earth, where moth and rust destroy, and where thieves break in and steal. But store up for yourselves treasures in heaven, where moth and rust do not destroy, and where thieves do not break in and steal. For where your treasure is, there your heart will be also."

From this passage of scripture and others, I have come to realize that the only lasting treasures are my relationships with God and with people. All the material things we acquire and all the other trophies we win will not last for eternity. They will pale compared to the riches of heaven. What we do on earth for Christ and others is what will last an eternity.

How then do we decide where to invest our time? I believe the answer is unique to each person. God created us as unique individuals with differing gifts and talents. I believe we each have unique talents that can be woven into the fabric of God's plan. As we develop an intimate relationship with God, He will reveal where He is working and show us where we can join Him in His work. When we join God in His work, we will experience Him. In their remarkable book, *Experiencing God: Knowing and Doing the Will of God*, Henry Blackaby and Claude King state that when God reveals His work to us, that is our invitation to join Him. As examples, they cited Noah and Moses, to whom God revealed His plan. Noah and Moses did not decide to build an ark or free the people of Israel. Rather, God revealed His plan to them and that was their invitation to join God where He is working. This is a clear guide to help us decide where to invest our limited time.

We are invited to join God where He is working when He reveals His work to us. Let me give you an example of how this has worked in my life. I live in a metropolitan area of more than 150,000 people. Thousands in this area do not know Jesus Christ as their Lord and Savior. This is an overwhelming need when compared to my limited time. Yet God is at work in many lives in our area. When I saw God working in the lives of eleven men, I experienced Him as I was privileged to disciple these men. (Not all at once, I might add.)

Before I began the discipleship program (Christian Businessmen's Connection, Operation *Timothy*), I saw God at work in their lives. I took that revelation as an invitation to join Him. As I have discipled these men, just as Charlie Fox discipled me, I experienced God in a most wonderful way. If you want to experience God in this way and store up treasures in heaven for yourself, join God where He reveals He is working.

What I have found in applying these Christian time stewardship principles is that they work together in harmony with each other and with God's plan. They do not compete against each other. For a truly balanced life, you will be doing all of these. For example, at one time I said yes to any and every invitation to participate in any Christian-related activity. As you can guess, I quickly became overcommitted.

For me to know where God wants me to invest my time using the unique talents He has given me, I must *spend time with Him.* I need to learn to recognize His voice so that I can make wise decisions. Before making a commitment, I try to spend time with God in prayer and listening to Him as He communicates to me through His Word, His Church, the Holy Spirit, and my circumstances. The greater the commitment, the more time I need to consider the commitment to be sure that my decision will please God. I try to consider if the commitment will be one that allows me to *demonstrate love for others.* I carefully *count the cost* to be sure I understand how much time I will be taking time away from something else. I try to be *faithful in even the little commitments of time,* because they will add up to a large amount of time and can have a major impact. Because a *faithful steward* takes care of all his flock, I want to make sure any new commitment does not prevent me from fulfilling other stewardship responsibilities. Because I cannot bear good fruit without Christ, I want to *live in harmony with God's plan.* These Christian time stewardship principles work together to give us the right balance in our lives. Yet there is another important principle that will be discussed in the next chapter.

# Application

By the time you finish this chapter, I hope you will spend time each day with God. As you grow closer to God, I believe that you will see where He is working in the world about you. Below, write any places where you see God at work around you. This might be the Holy Spirit touching the heart of a friend or relative or it might be a ministry like Gideons International.

During your quiet time with God, ask for wisdom as to what His direction is for you. For some of us, it may be to wait and prepare. Remember, Moses spent many years as a shepherd before he was called to lead the people of Israel out of Egypt. After I retired from the army, the very first thing I did was spend three days in fasting and prayer asking God to tell me His plan for me. I wanted to know His will. After reading scripture, praying, and talking with my pastor, I believe God wrote His thoughts on my mind as I neared the end of my three-day fast and was walking alone on a road near my house. God wrote on my heart these words: "Spend time with me."

That hit to the core of my heart. Here I was ready to serve Him, yet He knew what I needed most was to spend time with Him. Let me tell you that my obedience to spending time with Him brought me closer to Him and helped me see people and my situation through His eyes. Spending time with God has blessed me in many wonderful ways through my family, through two new careers, and now as a volunteer in retirement.

I suggest you spend time with God and then write down what you believe He wants you to do **to *live in harmony with His plan.***

# Key Verse

"Jesus said to them, 'My Father is always at his work to this very day, and I, too, am working'" (John 5:17).

# CHAPTER
# SEVEN

# Rest and Remember the Sabbath and Keep it Holy

A s you can readily discern, we all have many worthwhile activities that would benefit from an investment of our time. We could easily exhaust ourselves trying to meet all these worthwhile needs. This situation leads us to a seventh Christian time stewardship principle that can help guide a Christian's use of time: *rest*. Jesus recognized that His disciples needed rest. In Mark 6:31 Jesus said, "Come with me by yourselves to a quiet place and get some rest."

For me to rise at 5:30 a.m. to spend time with God, I need to go to bed at 10:30 p.m. so I can get adequate rest. I need seven hours of sleep each night. From my discussions with others, I believe the amount of sleep a person needs are unique. Each must determine the amount of sleep he or she needs to be refreshed. As you can see from my own example, I need seven hours. As my friend Bill Crisp tells me, "You cannot soar with the eagles in the morning if you hoot with the owls at night."

Throughout the Bible there are references to resting on the Sabbath and to keeping it holy. In Genesis 2:3 we read, "And God blessed the seventh day and made it holy, because on it he rested from all the work of creating that he had done."

Exodus 20:8–11 declares

> *Remember the Sabbath day by keeping it holy. Six days you shall labor and do all your work, but the seventh day is a Sabbath to the Lord your God. On it you shall not do any work, neither you, nor your son or daughter, nor your manservant or maidservant, nor your animals, nor the alien within your gates. For in six days the Lord made the heavens and the earth, the sea, and all that is in them, but he rested on the seventh day. Therefore,*

*the Lord blessed the Sabbath day and made*
*it holy.*

Jesus emphasized the fact that "The Sabbath was made for man, not man for the Sabbath" (Mark 2:27).

In recent years, our culture has experienced an exponential growth of available information and choices. The many opportunities and demands for our time seem to be endless. As I reflected on my own situation, I realized how much I needed to rest each day.

I realized how much I needed a Sabbath day when I could rest and spend time with God, my family, and with fellow Christians. For me this is Sunday. On this day of the week I can withdraw from the seemingly frantic pace of our society where everyone seems to be trying to put more and more activities into every minute. This phenomenon of increasing our activities is sometimes called multitasking or maximizing your time.

Now, I am not opposed to maximizing the use of our time. One of the ways is to rest and to worship God. I believe God created the Sabbath for us so that we will not wear ourselves out and so we can refresh ourselves through fellowship with Him. Just as a football coach gives rest to his players and encouragement on the sidelines, we need the rest and encouragement of a Sabbath day.

In Isaiah 58:13–14 we read, "'If you keep your feet from

breaking the Sabbath and from doing as you please on my holy day, if you call the Sabbath a delight and the Lord's holy day honorable, and if you honor it by not going your own way and not doing as you please or speaking idle words, then you will find your joy in the Lord, and I will cause you to ride on the heights of the land and to feast on the inheritance of your father Jacob.' The mouth of the Lord has spoken."

I believe that God's promised to Israel applies to us, His adopted sons and daughters, as well. I encourage you to *rest and remember the Sabbath and keep it Holy.*

I hope you will recognize that I began these seven principles by emphasizing the importance of spending time each day with God and that I have ended with rest and worship of our heavenly Father.

# Application

Reflect on the amount of rest you need each day to maintain yourself in good physical condition. In the space below, write out the number of hours of sleep you need each night to be adequately refreshed for the next day and how you plan to get adequate rest to meet your physical needs.

Now, turn your thoughts to the Sabbath. In the space below, write how you plan to apply the principle of keeping the Sabbath holy in your life.

# Key Verse

"Remember the Sabbath day by keeping it holy. Six days you shall labor and do all your work, but the seventh day is a Sabbath to the Lord your God. On it you shall not do any work, neither you, nor your son or daughter, nor your manservant or maidservant, nor your animals, nor the alien within your gates" (Exodus 20:8–10).

# Conclusion

God's Word revealed seven Christian time stewardship principles to me. I wish I could say that I spent all my first fifty years wisely following the seven Christian time stewardship principles described in this guide. Unfortunately, I can't. However, I am encouraged because I can apply them to the remaining portion of my life.

The Bible may contain more than these seven Christian time stewardship principles. I hope you will study scripture to know more of God and His ways and perhaps discover more time stewardship principles on your own.

The seven Christian time stewardship principles presented in this book can help us live balanced, fruitful lives that are pleasing to God. They complement each other and are in harmony with each other and God's plan for us.

The most important Christian time stewardship principle for me is *spending time with God*. He created us, knows us, and wants to have a personal relationship with us. As we spend time with Him, we will learn from Him. As we develop an intimate relationship with God, the Holy Spirit can lead us as our Good Shepherd in the day-to-day decisions that make up our lives. Jesus said, "I am the vine; you are the branches. If a man remains in me and I in him, he will bear much fruit; apart from me you can do nothing" (John 15:5). Through Christ's leading, we can live lives in harmony with God's plan and experience the abundant life.

My prayer for you and for myself is that one day we will hear these words from Jesus Christ, our Lord and Savior: "Well done, good and faithful servant! You have been faithful with a few things; I will put you in charge of many things. Come and share your master's happiness" (Matthew 25:21)!

# Appendix A

# Application and Time Log Worksheet

Although God does not change (Psalm 102:26–27; Romans 1:23; James 1:17), our world does. Over a large portion of the earth, many people live in a modern society characterized by sophisticated technology and information resources. It is a society that is quite different from the society described in the Old and New testaments of the Bible. Yet we must remember that God's Word does not change.

Consider, "The grass withers and the flowers fall, but the word of our God stands forever" (Isaiah 40:8). Therefore, we can take God's Word and apply it to our current situation. God's principles for living contained in His Word are immutable. They are appropriate yesterday, today, and tomorrow. Our human problem is how to apply

God's principles that are contained in His Word to the time in which we live on earth.

The application of God's principles to modern living requires us to consider the contemporary areas of stewardship responsibility most of us face. Some broad stewardship categories of modern life are suggested in the following paragraphs. These categories are areas that need an investment of our time so that we can live lives that are pleasing to our Lord and Savior, Jesus Christ.

**Relationship with God**: How much time am I spending on developing my relationship with the creator of the universe? How much time am I spending with God so that He can develop my character in the image of His Son, Jesus Christ? When was the last time that you read through the complete Bible? Do you spend as much time with the Bible each day as you do with the newspaper?

**People**: My family is my first responsibility. How much time am I investing in training my children and loving my wife or husband? How much time do I spend helping the needy and witnessing to others in the local and extended community?

**Resources**: Some examples of physical resources are property, such as cars, homes, money, and our physical bodies. Intangible resources include our time, training, and knowledge. Am I focusing on the resources as an end in themselves or on the stewardship of those resources to achieve what I perceive to be God's plan for me?

**Work**: How much time do I need to spend on my life's work? Am I becoming the best I can be at my life's work within the constraints of my other responsibilities?

**Self**: Am I meeting my physical, mental, social, and spiritual needs? Do my habits glorify God? In the final analysis, am I becoming the person of godly character that God intended me to be?

The legitimate claims on our time are in the final analysis unique to each person. The Time Log Worksheet that follows is another tool for your arsenal. Some people find it helpful to record the way they spend their time over a given period of a day or a week, so that they know how they are doing. You can use it to record your time by major categories of relationship with God, people, resources, work, and self or other categories of your own choosing.

Let me give you an example. Suppose you're concerned that you are not spending enough time with your family. You decide to record on Time Log Worksheets at the end of each day the amount of time you spent with each person in your family on that day. At the end of the week you add up the time you recorded on your worksheet. You can then compare the amount of time you want to spend with each person versus the time actually spent.

It has been said that the average American father

spends fewer than eight minutes per day in meaningful interaction with his children. How does that compare with our stewardship responsibility to train our children? I hope the enclosed Time Log Worksheet will assist you in *knowing how you are doing* with all the time, talent, and treasure God has entrusted in your care.

# Time for Christ: Time Log Worksheet

## Where am I spending my time?

Date:

Time:

People and other categories where I spend time

|  |  |  |  |  |  |  |
|--|--|--|--|--|--|--|
|  |  |  |  |  |  |  |
|  |  |  |  |  |  |  |
|  |  |  |  |  |  |  |
|  |  |  |  |  |  |  |
|  |  |  |  |  |  |  |
|  |  |  |  |  |  |  |
|  |  |  |  |  |  |  |
|  |  |  |  |  |  |  |
|  |  |  |  |  |  |  |
|  |  |  |  |  |  |  |
|  |  |  |  |  |  |  |
|  |  |  |  |  |  |  |
|  |  |  |  |  |  |  |
|  |  |  |  |  |  |  |
|  |  |  |  |  |  |  |
|  |  |  |  |  |  |  |

# Time for Christ: Time Log Worksheet

## Where am I spending my time?

Indicate in each square how much time you allotted in fifteen-minute increments. Elaborate on the activity, when possible.

Date:

|  | Sunday | Monday | Tuesday | Wednesday | Thursday | Friday | Saturday |
|---|---|---|---|---|---|---|---|
| Church |  |  |  |  |  |  |  |
| Family (name?) |  |  |  |  |  |  |  |
| Friends |  |  |  |  |  |  |  |
| Social (specify) |  |  |  |  |  |  |  |
| Activities |  |  |  |  |  |  |  |
| Other |  |  |  |  |  |  |  |
| Other |  |  |  |  |  |  |  |

# Appendix B

# Guide for Thinking about Christ-Pleasing Priorities

**Re: Money**

- Facts: although I have abundant money and possessions, they are limited.
- Needs: I can help those having less than me and even starving are vast, in my community, and in my nation, and especially in third-world countries.
- Scripture: Read Matthew 25:31–46 and Luke 6:27–31.
- Stewardship issues: How do I decide how much to give
  - o  to the church I am a member of?
  - o  to those I am responsible for?
  - o  for my personal needs?
  - o  for my personal desires?
  - o  to the vast numbers of poor and starving?

o  to charitable groups?

o  to personal evangelism, mission work?

## Re: Work Needing to Be Done

- Facts: I have limited abilities, skills; I cannot do everything. I do some things poorly and some things well. I have limited energy.
- Needs: I must determine that which no one is doing, that which not enough people are doing—that which is not being done well (or well enough).
- Scripture: Read Ecclesiastes 9:10; Philippians 2:12–13; Philippians 4:12–13.
- Stewardship issues: How do I balance out using myself up for God and God's work (above areas) and using myself sensibly for long term living and a helpful life? When should I accept tasks that appear beyond my own strength and abilities because they urgently need doing—relying on God's special, self-sufficient power?

## Re: Time

- Facts: I have a fixed amount of time each week 168 hours.
- Needs: There are vast numbers of legitimate claims on my own time.

- Scripture: Read Philippians 2:12–13; Philippians 4:12–13 .

- Stewardship issues: When is it appropriate and inappropriate to deprive others or myself of the time they have a legitimate claim on to do what I perceive as God's work for me?

# About the Author

D r. Gil Jacobs retired as dean of graduate studies and director of the Organizational Leadership Graduate Program at Mercyhurst University in May 2015.

Prior to joining Mercyhurst University, Dr. Jacobs earned his CPA license and worked for fourteen years as a CPA in industry serving as a vice president and comptroller for a steel manufacturing and erection company. Before his career in business, Dr. Jacobs served twenty-four years in the US Army and retired at the rank of lieutenant colonel in 1991. His military service included commanding infantry units in the United States and in combat in the Republic of Vietnam. He was an army ranger and master parachutist. He was commissioned an officer and awarded a Bachelor of Science degree from West Point in 1968; he earned a master's degree from the University of Central Texas in 1984 and a Doctor of Philosophy degree in organizational leadership and human resource development from Regent University, Virginia, in 2009.

He is happily married to Gail Jacobs. They have five adult children and ten grandchildren. They spend their time volunteering at First Alliance Church and with Gideons International. They recently returned from a short-term mission's trip in the Dominican Republic with Meeting-God-in-Missions, where they served on an optical team that provided eye glasses to Haitians who work in the sugarcane fields. He and Gail enjoy sailing, traveling, and visiting grandkids. Gil likes to stay physically active golfing, fishing, and hunting.

CPSIA information can be obtained
at www.ICGtesting.com
Printed in the USA
BVHW082128140819
555918BV00001B/15/P

9 781973 660422